D060200Z

HEDY
& HER AMAZING INVENTION

JAN WAHL illustrated by MORGANA WALLACE

penny
candy
BOOKS

Penny Candy Books

Oklahoma City & Savannah

Text © 2019 Jan Wahl

Illustrations © 2019 Morgana Wallace

All rights reserved. Published 2019. Printed in Canada.

 This book is printed on paper certified to the environmental and social standards of the Forest Stewardship Council™ (FSC®).

Portraits of Jan Wahl & Morgana Wallace: Morgana Wallace
Design: Shanna Compton

23 22 21 20 19   1 2 3 4 5
ISBN-13: 978-0-9987999-9-5 (hardcover)

Small press. Big conversations.
www.pennycandybooks.com

TO MARY DAWSON

CHAPTER 1

There is a technology we use every day in our cell phones, microwaves, alarm systems, laptop computers, and many other things. How did it get invented? A fascinating question.

Well, once there was a glamorous movie star named Hedy—her face was known everywhere. She was whip smart, someone who demanded to know how everything worked. This is her story.

She was born Hedwig Kiesler in the city of Vienna, in Austria—the same year that World War I started, 1914. The war was a brutal one, with terrible fighting taking place in Europe. In 1918, when it was over, many in Austria lived in poverty. But almost everybody could go to the movies. A ticket only cost a few coins.

On Hedy's fourth birthday she rode with her father on a streetcar into the center of the city. Herr Kiesler, a banker, had taken the afternoon off. Her father took Hedy to the Kino, a movie theater where they saw *The Pied Piper of Hamelin*. What she liked best were the rats made of wood, scampering and dashing madly.

Afterwards she asked, "How do pictures get on the screen?" He told her about projectors. How they shine light through film invented by an American, George Eastman. And they rode home, Hedy thinking all the way. When they got there, her father gave her a present.

It was a gold watch, round and shiny. What made those tiny wheels spin? Instead of eating, Hedy wanted to pull it apart to see how it worked. Her mother said, "For goodness sake, eat your dinner. Don't break your new watch."

CHAPTER 2

Hedy acted all the time. She watched grownups and had fun copying them. She imitated her mother, the cook, and the postman. Everyone knew whom she was copying just by the way she walked. In the garden, under a rose arbor, she acted out fairy tales and movie stories. Her father said, "Ever since you were a baby you've been an actress. Hold onto your dreams and they'll come true!"

Her mother, Frau Kiesler, hoped her daughter would be a pianist like herself. Hedy was good at playing the piano, but she hated all the practicing. Secretly, up in her room, she invented a new soda pop. A bottle exploded. Her mother was upset. "Oh well," Hedy said to calm her, "I've got other projects." She was no longer a little child.

Her mother said, "You may as well go on the stage. That would be safer! You will learn to speak nicely and wear elegant costumes." So her parents let her attend acting classes. Instead, she often sneaked away to movie

studios to watch that mysterious business. People were already noticing how she looked. However, Hedy wanted to be more than just a pretty girl.

As a teenager she began acting professionally in the theater. Night after night, in the same play, she had to speak the same words. It was boring. Hedy started to like movies more than theater. Every story and each day was different. And when she made movies, she saw her picture on posters—not only in Vienna but all over Europe.

CHAPTER 3

Her parents worried. Such a life for a well-brought-up Jewish girl! She agreed to go out with an older man named Fritz Mandl, who talked about interesting things. He filled her parents' home with flowers. One afternoon he took Hedy driving in the great park of Vienna. A faraway band played waltzes, and he asked her to marry him. Hedy accepted.

Herr Mandl bought her jewels and furs, but she preferred to visit his factories. Hedy studied the machines, trying to figure out how they worked. Yet she hated the objects that were made—weapons for war. At dinner parties she sat listening to visitors talk about many things, including torpedoes. The men believed she didn't understand, but she was paying attention.

Herr Mandl did not wish Hedy to continue acting. She asked might she have a small space of her own, in which she could try to make things. He replied, "That isn't proper! You are my princess—this is my castle!"

Now she realized she was a prisoner. There was a whole world beyond those walls with much to discover. Then—suddenly—her father died, and she felt alone. It was necessary to escape. So one night Hedy crept away, taking a few clothes and a paper bag of jewels.

Hedy left by bicycle for the train station. She journeyed, by train and by boat, to London. There Hedy met Mr. Mayer of Metro-Goldwyn-Mayer in Hollywood, who offered her a contract for $125 a week. She said no.

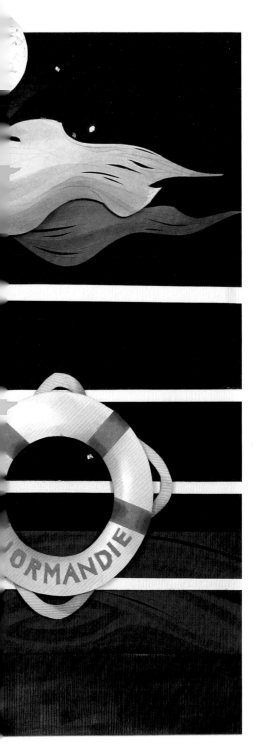

CHAPTER 4

Instead, Hedy had an idea. She bought a ticket for America on the *Normandie*, the largest ship afloat, the ship on which Mr. Mayer was returning home. Every evening, on deck, she wore her most elegant gown. Louis B. Mayer couldn't help paying attention. At dinner he offered a better contract. And Mrs. Mayer declared, "We will call you Hedy Lamarr."

In Hollywood, they knew best how to photograph and to light her—creating an MGM star. She posed for what she felt were silly photos. Magazines informed readers she was the "World's Most Beautiful Woman." Still, being a star was not satisfying enough.

Sometimes she was expected to wear a movie costume too gaudy, too heavy, or just plain unwearable. So she took it home, adjusting it herself secretly. She was not permitted to change words in a script, yet at least she felt better.

At home, Hedy set up a strong lamp on a work table with equipment of all kinds. She invented a new Kleenex box. And a dog collar that would light up so you could find a lost pet in the dark. MGM didn't know she had another life.

World War II was starting. Germany invaded Poland and Czechoslovakia. Hedy worried about her mother back in Vienna, for Adolph Hitler had seized Austria as part of Nazi Germany. The Germans set fire to London. Hedy lay in bed at night imagining the horror of it.

Nazi submarines were sinking British ships. England needed help desperately. It fought back with radio-controlled torpedoes. Germans jammed the radio signals so British torpedoes did not reach Nazi submarines. Hedy wanted to invent a way to outsmart the jamming of signals, to let the British strike German targets. She had to find the answer!

CHAPTER 5

One day, to relax, Hedy went to a party where she met the composer George Antheil. Together they sat at the piano. George would play a melody at his end of the keyboard—next Hedy would repeat it or play against it. To fool each other, they'd switch keys.

Suddenly she stopped and lifted her fingers from the keyboard. She remembered her husband talking about wireless communication. If music notes can move from octave to octave, or key to key, you can move a radio signal from frequency to frequency!

The following morning she told George her idea. He nodded, saying, "There are 88 keys on the piano...Look! What about 88 frequencies? We can put something like player-piano rolls into your torpedoes."

(A player-piano is automated and plays without anyone pressing any keys. Keys move by a system using paper rolls with holes punched in them. Where holes are

punched decides which notes play on the keyboard.)

    He continued, "Then both transmitter and receiver stay on the same frequency. It won't matter how fast the frequency changes."

CHAPTER 6

Every evening for weeks the two worked together. They lay on the living room floor like kids—using a silver matchbox and wooden matches. The matchbox was a Nazi submarine, the matches were the torpedoes. At the studio she never mentioned what she worked on at home.

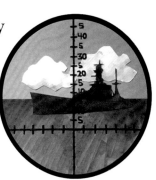

Hedy called her invention "frequency hopping." George helped get it written up. When the blueprints were ready, he took the patent application to Washington. This was 1941, the U.S.A. had not yet entered the fight. Hedy waited anxiously for the patent. It was difficult to concentrate on movie work.

The patent was granted a year later, after the Japanese bombed Pearl Harbor. However, the U.S. Navy, to whom Hedy gave her patent, decided the invention was not practical, and they put it on hold. Her disappointment was great, yet what she didn't know was that her invention would change the day-to-day world we all live in.

Her mother managed to escape from Austria to England. At last Hedy was able to bring her to America—to stay in comfort until the end of her days. Frau Kiesler brought old country recipes, including Hedy's favorite, cabbage soup with spaetzle. Hedy often brought pots of it to share at the studio.

Hedy had a substantial movie career, though she found some of her roles to be absurd. In the high-budget *Ziegfeld Girl* she wore a preposterous headdress towering high up in the air. It was fastened to her neck and back. She ached for a week.

When showman Cecil B. DeMille made his Technicolor Bible epic, *Samson and Delilah*, Hedy played Delilah in an ornate peacock gown with a long, long train trailing behind her. She was happy to rush home to wear a cotton skirt and a sloppy pullover. In her workshop she continued to invent.

CHAPTER 7

Time passed. In 1962, John Kennedy was president. And Russia built threatening missile sites close to Florida, in Cuba. Hedy's frequency hopping or "spread spectrum" now got dusted off to make foolproof torpedoes. Instead of punched paper rolls, it used transistors. The Cuban missile crisis ended because Cuba was blockaded successfully by American warships and submarines that carried Hedy's torpedoes.

A patent is good for twenty years. And since 1962, her invention has been employed in many ways—in industry, in science, in medicine. It is used in software, alarm systems, portable laptop computers, microwaves, cell phones, GPS, Wi-Fi, Bluetooth, barcode scanning, wireless Internet, satellite-guided missiles, and a lot more.

Even as an old lady, Hedy kept inventing. She had a plan for a better traffic light, as well as improvements for the French super jet, the Concorde. And on March 20, 1997 the Electronics Frontier Foundation officially awarded its Frontier Award "To Hedy Lamarr for Her Contribution in Pioneering Electronics."

She was 82. She decided to stay home, recording a message of thanks on tape. In honor of this wonderful woman, Hedy's birthday—November 9th—is celebrated around the world as Inventors' Day.

I was to meet Hedy Lamarr three times in my life. Once at Hammer Galleries on 57th Street in New York. She stood there in the middle of it all, not as a famous movie star, but strictly as a painter. The paintings on the gallery walls were delightful abstract works. She was gracious and still glamorous—eager to speak with anyone not about the past, only about what was happening: her colorful creations.

Another time was in Colorado one blustery, near-blizzardy afternoon. She and her then husband were considering purchasing motels in the mountains—cozy Austrian-inspired chalets for the tourists who came to ski. With a twinkle in her eye she declared she intended to call her motels "Hedy's Beddies."

The final occasion was in Mexico City at a party for the great Mexican poet Octavio Paz. One guest most eager to meet him, Miss Lamarr, had just had surgery. She herself removed the bandages that very morning. "Nothing was going to stop me!" she declared—not attempting to hide behind dark glasses. To my surprise she recited one of his short poems in perfect Spanish. Señor Paz was tickled pink.

BIBLIOGRAPHY

Barton, Ruth. *HEDY LAMARR, The Most Beautiful Woman on Film.* The University Press of Kentucky. 2010.

Lamarr, Hedy. *Ecstasy and Me.* Fawcett. 1966.

Rhodes, Richard. *HEDY'S FOLLY, The Life and Breakthrough Inventions of Hedy Lamarr, The Most Beautiful Woman in the World.* Doubleday. 2012.

Robbins, Trina. *Hedy Lamarr and a Secret Communication System.* Capstone Press. 2007.

Shearer, Stephen Michael. *BEAUTIFUL, The Life of Hedy Lamarr.* St. Martin's Press. 2010.

Young, Christopher. *The Films of Hedy Lamarr.* Citadel Press. 1987.

JAN WAHL is the author of over one hundred children's books, including the Coretta Scott King Honor-winner *Little Eight John* and the Christopher Medal-winner *Humphrey's Bear*. Bowling Green State University has awarded him the honorary degree of Doctor of Letters in recognition of his continuing work in children's literature and in the history of film. Jan lives and writes in Toledo, OH.

MORGANA WALLACE was born into an artistic family in Winnipeg, Manitoba, and later moved to Victoria, British Columbia, where she studied at the Victoria College of Art before becoming a full-time artist. As a child, she was captivated by book illustrations and still believes they are as important as the narrative. Her medium is mainly paper collage, but she incorporates watercolor, ink, and pen to create her imaginary world of characters.